Handmade POTTERY AT HOME

Handmade POTTERY AT HOME

SIMPLE CERAMICS TO MAKE ON YOUR KITCHEN TABLE

Frida Anthin Broberg

Photography: Andreas Hylthén

D&C
David and Charles

www.stitchcraftcreate.co.uk

Pottery my way

This is a book about pottery done my way. I want it to convey and express my uncomplicated love for creation and pottery while hopefully inspiring both young and old clay enthusiasts.

You don't need any prior experience in order to follow the step-by-step instructions in this book. Nor do you need many tools. A piece of cloth, a rolling pin and some plastic wrap will go a very long way. However, you will need access to a kiln. Perhaps you are following a course where a kiln is available, or you could get in touch with your local potter and ask if you might use a corner of their kiln at the next firing. You could, of course, be fortunate enough to have your own kiln.

All pottery and all templates in this book are made and designed by me in my workshop. Photos are by Andreas Hylthén. At the end you will find some facts and a glossary which might be helpful in case there is something you are unfamiliar with.

Feel free to be inspired!

Frida

Contents

textile memories

There are forgotten treasures in Granny's attic.
Crocheted tablecloths can find new life as
patterns on a coffee cup.

Inspired by fabric

Every Christmas when I was a little girl, I peeped at the small, soft parcels under the Christmas tree, carefully wrapped in recycled paper by my Granny, Majken.

The parcel might contain an unfashionable knitted jumper or a batik tablecloth which Granny had bought in Ceylon when she was a missionary, but more often it was an item that Granny had crocheted. Dainty armrest covers, a small pot-holder or starched little table mats to put the finest ornaments on.

Granny had a dresser in her home filled with these textiles, and every Christmas she dug out some Christmas presents for us grandchildren. It was almost magical, that dresser, because the drawers seemed bottomless – and I opened my Christmas presents without much enthusiasm.

Years have gone by and, sadly, Granny is no more. Nevertheless, she lives on in my memory and in my arsenal of crocheted tablecloths.

Since I do not use a lot of tablecloths at home, they have mostly survived by being stowed away. These fine crocheted creations with advanced star patterns and lovely flowers have been lying there waiting for me. When one day I started working with pottery and pressed textile designs into clay, I had the idea of using Granny's items – so now we work together, she and I!

Curtains, embroidered tablecloths, crocheted ribbons, lace and linens with monograms – yes, everything can be pressed and immortalized in pottery.

11

1

The finest lace curtain leaves a delicate and romantic design in the clay.

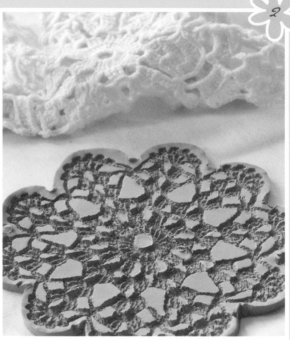

2

Round crocheted table mats are perfect for pressing into dishes and bowls.

3

Roll different ribbons into the clay and cut out the patterns – you get nice decorations to attach around cups and pots.

Some tips on textiles

Anybody who has not had the privilege of opening soft parcels with crocheted tablecloths and mats every Christmas can find textile craft bargains at flea markets.

When pressing textiles into pottery, remember that the coarser the structure of the textile pattern, the clearer the impression will be in the clay. Crocheted tablecloths and mats and crocheted ribbons produce more robust patterns, while lace curtains leave a finer, more superficial pattern.

Put the crocheted tablecloth or mat on the rolled clay and roll into the cloth firmly before carefully lifting it off. If the clay is too wet, the mat will stick and the pattern becomes blurred. In this case, use a hairdryer or wait a while before you roll the mat in for a perfect result.

It is simpler to roll in an entire pattern over the whole clay plate and to cut out the pieces according to the template afterwards. Sometimes you will want to know exactly where the pattern will end up, and then you can do the pressing after cutting out the shapes. The shape might change a little because of the pressure you apply, so it's best to re-apply the template and cut where needed to tidy up the edges.

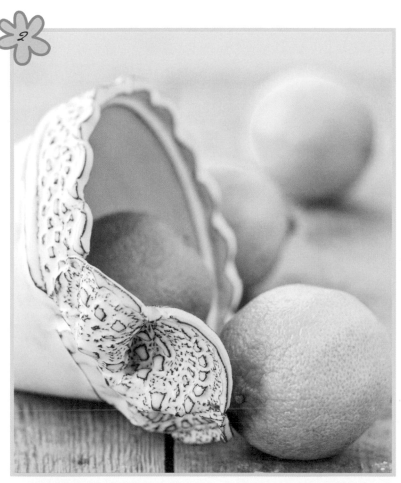

 Edge decoration created with patterns from various crocheted ribbons.

 Small pot with pleated decoration of crocheted ribbon.

 Jug with pattern from lace curtains.

 Plate with pattern from a crocheted tablecloth.

Make your own

Make your own

Here I show you step by step how to make a coffee cup using a pattern from crocheted ribbons. Templates can be found on page 19.

Roll the textile into the clay or press it in with your fingers. Re-cut the pieces following the template if the shape has changed because of the pressure you applied. If the clay is very wet and difficult to lift, dry it a little with a hairdryer or let it rest for a while.

Roll the clay into a slab, which should be about 3mm (⅛in) thick. Cut out the pieces according to the template.

Use a fork or another tool to score the edges before joining them.

Apply slip to the scored edges and press together. Tidy the joints with a knife.

Roll a small band with crochet pattern. Score the reverse of the band and the cup where the ribbon should be. Apply slip and fasten it around the cup. Tidy up with a damp sponge and leave to dry under plastic wrap.

Score around the round bottom part, inside the cup and on the foot. Apply slip and join all three parts. Finally, score the ends of the handle and the area on the cup where the handle will be attached, apply slip and press together. Tidy up the joints.

Cup template

A template is given opposite for a coffee cup with a foot. Roll the clay and use your finest crocheted ribbons to create the pattern.

I fastened a decorative ribbon onto the cup. Roll a thin strip of clay and press a beautiful, crocheted ribbon into it. Cut out the pattern from the clay.

1 side

3 foot

bottom 4

2 handle

tip!

Roll out the clay on textile and turn several times while rolling so that the slab becomes nice and even.

Discovering decals

Roses are red, violets are blue… In the world of decals flowers can bloom in any colour you like.

Red rose delights

I first became aware of decals when I trained as a crafts teacher and did an internship at an open pottery workshop. One day I had the chance to accompany the manager to a large pottery wholesaler.
And there they were – the decals.

Pink roses with pale green leaves were my first ever decals. They adorned my very first wheel-thrown cups – cups that are still used today.

Well, at least the roses match....

Some people think decals are too simple; in fact, that they are almost cheating. They think hand painting is best. Since I love cheating and shortcuts, and neither have the patience nor the skill required for hand painting, I have totally abandoned myself to the world of decals. I can sit for hours and browse long lists of roses, butterflies, angels and deer in the web shops. I love it!

psst ...

There is no cup, vase, jug or plate that cannot be decorated with a decal – or several!

1

Choose your decals and cut out the shape you want.

2

Let them soak in a bowl of water until they peel from the paper.

3

Apply the decals on the piece of pottery.

Some tips on decals

Decals are ready-made patterns that can be applied to finished pieces and burned into the glaze. There are a number of retailers on the internet and decals are cheap to buy.

Decals are attached to a paper backing and must be soaked for several minutes until they peel. A protective, transparent paper may also be attached to the decal and this must be removed before soaking.

When the decals are floating in the bowl with water, you might feel unsure about which is the front and which is the reverse of the design. As a rule, the side that is more matt is the reverse and the side that should face the pottery.

Cut your decals any way you like. You can cut letters and figures from sheets of decals. Large decals can be cut into half, while small ones look nice in a cluster.

Put them in a bowl with water, several at a time. After a couple of minutes, the decals will rise to the surface. Place the decals on the piece. You have plenty of time: the decals will not stick immediately, so you can take your time moving them around until you are happy with their position.

Use a soft sponge and be careful to remove any air bubbles. Leave to dry and refire the piece in a kiln at about 800 degrees.

Favourite cup with a mix of small decals, plus a large rose decal cut into three parts.

Large cup with large decal roses and matching saucer.

There are entire decal sheets available with dots in various colours. Mix with roses to get a really romantic look.

These cups have been dipped in blue glaze and decorated with blue roses cut in half.

Make your own ≫

Make your own

Here I show you step by step how to make a large cup with a squiggly handle. Templates can be found on page 33.

Press the rolled slab down into the bowl and press against the edges. Tidy up with a damp sponge.

Roll out a slab 3mm (⅛in) thick. Line a small bowl of a suitable shape with plastic wrap.

Cut along the edge of the bowl and remove the excess. Leave to dry or blow-dry the inside of the bowl for a few minutes with a hairdryer.

Score the area on the cup where the handle will be attached and apply slip. Press firmly and add a little support in the form of a piece of paper below the handle. Tidy the edge with a damp sponge. Leave to dry under plastic.

Roll out a long strip of clay, about 5mm (¼in) thick. Cut out a handle in two parts following the template and form the pointed ends into scrolls.

Cut the ends diagonally. Score and apply slip on the ends. Attach the little squiggly part of the handle on to the big part.

31

Follow the step-by-step instructions
on the previous page.

Cup template

Here are some templates for the squiggly handle for the large cup.
Turn the cup or roll out the clay and use a bowl as a mould.

1 Handle

2 Small handle detail

tip!

There are many ways of making a handle. Decorate it with multiple details and you get a personalized cup.

Impressed with imprints

To plant a seed and watch it grow is almost a magical experience. Imagine being able to do so using a ceramic pot you made yourself!

Garden memories

I grew up in an adult education college where my father was a teacher. For fifteen years, we lived in a small house on the college campus. In the summer, I often woke up to hear a pleasant humming noise. The gardener, Yngve, was cutting the grass right outside my window. Flowerbeds were weeded and trees cut.

I drove my dolls around in surroundings that were like a park. Sometimes I ventured down to Yngve's workshop, in the basement of one of the college buildings. It smelt so nice down there, I thought – a mixture of gasoline and soot. Yngve knew exactly why I was there. He had a metal shelf with loads of small boxes and would pick out some candy from one of them.

These days I live with my family in a small farmhouse. When we moved here there was a garden landscaped by pensioners who took a very great interest in gardening. There were rows of flowerbeds in bloom throughout the season, with rose bushes and carefully arranged groups of flowers around the entire house. Rumour had it that they cut the grass with scissors by hand!

There is no Yngve who hums past in the morning or who weeds the flowerbeds, for that matter. Nowadays gravel surrounds our house and the flowerbeds are mostly full of bishop's weed. Even so, each summer I do try to cultivate plants in a few pots, and dream about both a greenhouse and a herb garden.

In the forest and around the corner – everywhere there are beautiful objects and plants that can be pressed into clay.

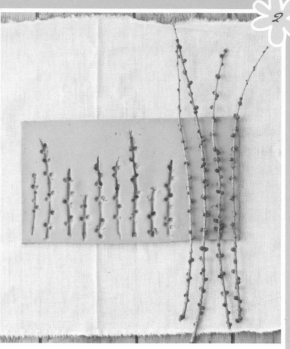

Use real flowers or flowers made of plastic and roll into the clay.

Larch tree twigs produce nice-looking patterns.

A few rusty keys will leave clear imprints.

Leaves with strong veining produce fantastic texture.

Some tips on imprints

Look around in nature and in your drawers at home and you will find a range of objects that you can use to make imprints in clay. I have used branches, leaves and flowers. Old keys leave fantastic patterns and you might find ready-made stamps in children's toy boxes that you can use.

The pattern will be more or less visible depending on the colour of the clay. I have used both white and dark clay in this chapter.

Roll out a slab of clay. If it's very wet, blow-dry it with a hairdryer. For example, place a leaf on the clay, roll it in and then lift away the leaf. If a piece of the leaf breaks off and gets stuck in the clay, it can stay, as it will burn away in the kiln.

If you are shaping a piece by turning it on a wheel, it can be difficult to press your pattern into it without warping the piece. Let the turned piece dry a little and get a little steadier before you press. Press with your fingers.

You can also roll out the decoration separately. Cut out and fasten it with slip and then tidy the joints.

 A slab with an imprint of a key is a nice decoration to hang on a door.

 Rolled-in leaves look pretty in the garden.

 Plant labels in Italian. These will spruce up any herb pot!

 Herb pots with imprints of thyme and small feet.

Make your own ≫

Make your own

Follow these step-by-step instructions and you will soon have your own pot to sow a few seeds in. Templates can be found on page 47.

Roll out the clay on a piece of cloth. Turn several times while rolling so that the slab becomes nice and even. Cut out the parts of the template in the clay.

Choose a nice twig, flower or leaf as decoration. Here I used a small twig of thyme. Roll it in and then lift it away.

Score the side and bottom and join together using slip.

4

Make an even clay roll. Cut it into four equal parts, each about 2cm (¾in) long.

5

Form the parts into little feet.

6

Score the feet and also the area below the pot where the feet will be attached. Fix with slip.

↰ Follow the step-by-step instructions on the previous page.

Herb pot template

Use the templates to make a small pot for the kitchen window. Why not make several? Oregano, rosemary and basil all leave nice imprints.

You can form the feet as you like, or skip them. If you want a pot with drainage holes, make holes in the bottom. Turn or roll out a plate and put feet on that instead!

 *side*

Make this template x 2

2

bottom

tip! Remember that the shape may change when you press a pattern into it. Replace the template on the clay and cut again for the best result.

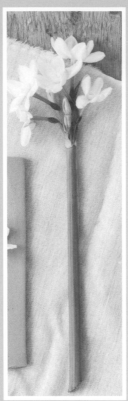

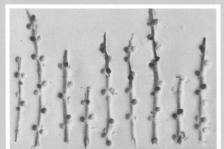

Glistening glazes

The magnolia has existed for twenty million years. When it blooms, it is as if time stands still.

Cottage life

Is there anything more idyllic than a small cottage in the countryside? Imagine it in summer in a small clearing in the forest. Or perhaps by a lake with a rickety jetty. So many possibilities… Calm waters and a moored rowing boat. Horse pastures with buttercups. The smell of freshly mown hay, summer rain and lily of the valley. Freshly washed sheets blowing in the wind.

We set the table in the lilac arbour with strawberry squash and cinnamon buns. Stretch our toes in the grass and read a book under the apple tree.

In the evening, we open the door to the cottage. It is painted golden ochre. The handle is cold and the key a little stiff. Inside are rag rugs and floorboards. We make coffee on the wood stove, while the cat weaves around our legs. Perhaps we might sit in the rocking chair and watch night fall. Later we crawl into bed between the wind-scented sheets with the cat to keep us company. When the sun rises, we stretch, and maybe fall back to sleep. There is no clock at the cottage.

Everyone should have a small cottage, if not in reality, at least mentally. Somewhere to go when the stress of everyday life takes over.

Engobe in old honey jars. Brushes and sponges
are great to have around for engobing.

Place your pattern on top and gently carve the contours. I used a magnolia cut out of left-over wallpaper. Use a sponge-stick to add some colour where you see fit. I used pink and green engobe.

Carve out your template design with a sharp tool.

Roll on a primer. Here I used white engobe. Roll twice if you want the paint to cover.

Some tips on engobing

Engobe is a coloured liquid clay slip which is used below clear glazing. Engobe is used mainly for pieces that are fired at earthenware temperatures. Pieces must be sturdy and leather-hard, in other words they are not bisque-fired. Once engobed, leave to dry and bisque-fire. Afterwards, dip into a clear glaze and glaze-fire.

Engobe is available in all colours imaginable. You can buy it ready-mixed from your clay wholesale supplier, but it's just as simple, and cheaper, to buy engobe powder and mix it with water. Engobe should have the consistency of heavy cream. If you make a lot of engobe, you can dip the entire piece into it.

In this chapter I used white, pink and green engobe. I used a foam roller, brushes of different widths, sponge-sticks and a tool with a round tip which I use to carve patterns. First, roll on an even layer of engobe on your piece. Let it dry a little and roll another layer on. Use a brush for places you cannot reach, such as around handles. If you want to use different colours, let the engobe dry a little between layers. Use a template or a pattern and carefully mark where the pattern should appear on your piece. Use a brush or a sponge -stick to colour specific sections. You will have to carve last if you don't want the paint to get into the lines.

Small bowl brushed inside with white engobe. Pot with white engobe and carved magnolias.

Fancy hangers with small magnolias. Rolled, cut out and engobed in white, pink and green. The pattern is carved at the end.

Small decorative wall plate with two holes along the lower edge for combined hanging and hook function. Perfect for necklaces or evening shoes.

Rolled jugs with magnolias. I rolled on white engobe as a primer. Pink and green engobe are applied with a sponge-stick and then finally the pattern is carved.

Make your own »

Make your own

Would you like to make a jug for your magnolias or perhaps another favourite flower? Follow my step-by-step instructions. Templates can be found on page 61.

Score both the sides and around the bottom part. Apply slip and press together.

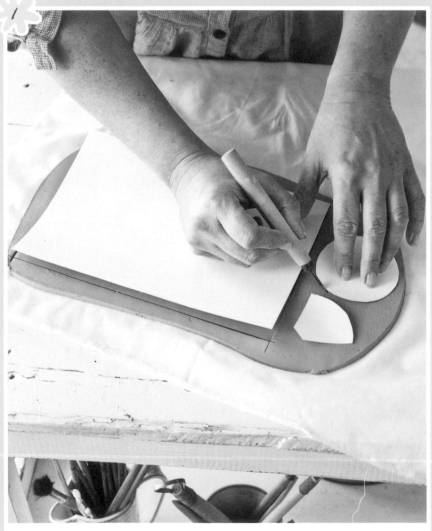

Roll out the clay as evenly as possible on a piece of cloth. Place the templates on top and cut out the parts in the clay.

Form the spout and score the edges. Also score the area on the jug where the spout should be attached. Attach with slip.

Cut out an opening for the spout on the inside of the jug.

Make an even roll of clay, flatten it a little and form into a handle.

Score the ends of the handle and the clay where you want to attach the handle on the jug. Apply slip and press the handle into the jug. Use a support below the handle so that it does not come off while drying. Cover with plastic.

Jug template

Enlarge or reduce
the template if you
want the jug to be a
different size. Make
a handle from a clay
roll or roll a thick
slab and cut out.

Leave the jug to dry
until it's leather-dry
and then brush or
dip in engobe. Carve
nice patterns.

 side

Make this template x 2

spout

2

3

bottom

tip! It looks good if the spout is rolled a little thinner than the jug. Bend it directly to prevent the clay from cracking.

test treasures

They say the way to a man's heart is through his stomach. That applies to dogs and children as well. Not least to mine.

Food fantasies

I have travelled to few countries, but I have eaten my way around the world. After many childhood years spent in the countryside, I moved to a big city. A whole new world of flavours opened up.

I remember so well the first time I was invited to a fine restaurant. The restaurant was perched high up and had a view over large parts of the city. I sat at the bar and pretended to be relaxed while I waited. The waiters wore nice clothes, weaved quickly between the tables and were rude. They probably saw through me straight away, saw that it was the first time I had been in a fine restaurant. In order to prove the opposite, I ordered the most expensive thing they had on the menu – oysters. This was a fatal move. I didn't even know how to eat them and thought they tasted terrible. My first time in a fine restaurant could certainly have been more successful. After the bill came, no more dinners followed with that particular date.

That was back then, but now I eat everything. It is an understatement to say that I love food. My husband cooks the finest dishes, and there is no better way to socialize than over dinner, preferably in a messy, hot kitchen, at a rustic table set with ceramics and with flavours from all over the world.

psst …

Stamps with letters can be used for so much. Not least on pottery. You can write anything, a poem or a name, and voilà! – a bowl with character.

BON APPE TIT

1

BON aP Pe TiT

2

Bon appetit

3

Some tips on text and pottery

I like to put text on my pottery; usually I stamp names on children's sets. But there are so many other things you can do with text and pottery. The theme of this chapter is the kitchen. There are so many things in the kitchen that you can put text on. Small labels for the jars in the larder. Signs for kitchen towels. Name tags for the table and napkin rings bidding you welcome. Bowls, dishes and cups can always do with a line of text, in my opinion.

You can find stamps in many shops. Any material will do – rubber, wood or metal. You can buy paper letters to roll into clay, but you can always make your own by writing text on thick cardboard and cutting them out. You can print by hand with a tool or a pencil with a round tip.

The clay should not be too wet when you print on it. Let it dry a little or blow-dry with a hairdryer for a short while. The clay must also not be too dry. If you want to stamp on wheel-thrown pieces, it is particularly important for the clay to harden a little before you press the letters into it. Hold one hand as a support inside the piece and press gently.

 I used paper letters which I rolled in and then lifted away.

 By mixing large and small letters on stamps, you get a playful look.

 Write by hand to achieve a more personal feel.

 Soupe du jour. Soup of the day. Printed by hand.

 Le lait. Milk. Don't forget the biscuits! Printed with stamps.

 Serviette. Text on a simple napkin ring.

 Cuisine. Kitchen. A pretty sign for the kitchen shelf. Here I used paper letters which I rolled in and then lifted away.

Make your own ≫

Make your own

The most delightful bowl. Follow my step-by-step instructions and soon you will have a new bowl for your best friend. Templates can be found on page 75. Remember that when you press text on the side, the shape may change; place the template over the item again to make sure the bowl is even.

Print by pressing or rolling in letters in the clay. I used paper letters which I rolled in and then lifted away.

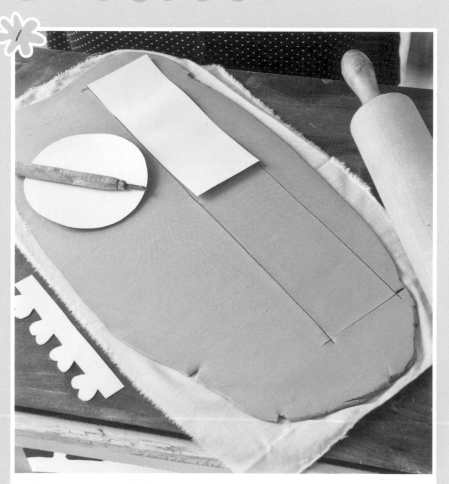

Roll out an even slab of clay on a piece of cloth. Cut out the parts of the template in the clay.

Score the edges on the sides and around the bottom. Apply slip and press together. Tidy the joints.

Roll out a long slab of clay. Cut according to the edge decoration template with a small knife.

Score around the entire edge of the bowl and on the decoration. Apply slip and press together.

Tidy all joints and the decoration with a sponge.

Follow the step-by-step instructions on the previous page.

Dog bowl template

Here are the templates for the dog bowl. The bowl is suitable for a small dog, so if your dog is large, you may need to enlarge the template.

Britney also has a ceramic B attached to the dog collar – for special occasions.

 *side*

Make this template x 2

| 20cm (8in) | 20cm (8in) |

8cm (3in)

2 *bottom*

3 *edge decor*

tip!

It's a little tricky to cut out the decoration. Use my template or draw your own. Tidy using a sponge.

Cookie cutter creations

Chestnuts roasting on an open fire,
Jack Frost nipping at your nose,
Yuletide carols being sung by a choir,
and folks dressed up like Eskimos.

Shapely creations

Easy-peasy, I thought, the first time I tried working with clay. Of course it was easy, I had discovered cookie cutters. I was sitting in a drop-in workshop, cutting out perfect shapes which I pressed together to make small votives – the votives on the picture at the beginning of this chapter. I was so pleased with my discovery that I continued to produce cookie-cutter pottery. Advent candle holders and Christmas tree pendants, garlands and candle decorations. Pottery was really easy-peasy.

Later I tried throwing pieces on a potter's wheel. This was not as easy. Still, I could cut out pretty decorations with my cookie cutters and camouflage all my lopsided bowls and plates with them. So I was happy again.

Nowadays I mostly use the cookie cutters for Christmas, but I always bring a few if I work with children. Cutters are suitable for all beginners and it's almost impossible to fail. If children have difficulty concentrating, cookie cutters are perfect, since you get a good result quickly.

Children are wonderfully talented and natural when it comes to creating. They immediately start to shape, press and fantasize. Children are my greatest source of inspiration, and I often bring back their solutions and ideas to my workshop. Together with the cookie cutters, of course!

These days you can find cookie cutters with fantastic shapes. Princess crowns, animals from all over the world and my favourite – the snow star!

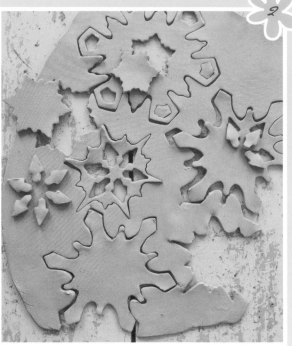

Cut out a snow star. Here I used a cookie cutter made of several parts. Each as unique as the original. Cut out the shape with a large cutter and press various shapes inside with the smaller cutters.

The snow star can hang anywhere – on the Christmas tree, on a door or on the finest Christmas present.

Let the snow star dry with a flat weight on top so that it does not warp.

Some tips on cookie cutters

Next time you're standing there holding a cookie cutter in your hand and wondering whether or not you need it – buy it! The cutters are perfect for pottery. If you search the Internet, you can find almost any shape. The American cookie cutter market is huge.

Here is what to do. Roll out a slab of clay on a piece of cloth, nice and evenly, and press your cutters down. If you are making hanging ornaments, let them dry under a weight so they don't warp during the drying process. Don't forget to make a hole for the string. The shape will shrink when it dries, so remember not to make the hole too small.

If you want to make decorations to attach to another shape, apply slip on the reverse and press together. If you are attaching several shapes in a row, it's best to score the area a little, apply slip and press together so that they do not come apart during the drying process.

The theme in this chapter is Christmas; however, lots of items made with cookie cutters can be used all year round.

I have a box full of cookie cutters which I bought in America. Numbers and letters. The numbers 1-4 are great for candles during Advent.

Some hearts with holes in them make a lovely garland. Attach them to a pretty piece of string and hang in the window.

Beautifully wrapped parcels look wonderful under the Christmas tree. Decorate them with small ceramic pendants. Little old men and women also make pretty Christmas tree decorations.

Advent candle holder with small stars. On the next page I will show you how to make one. Replace the stars with hearts or perhaps numbers for a bit of variety.

Make your own »

Make your own

The Advent candle holder with small stars cut out with a cookie cutter is very easy to make. Follow my step-by-step instructions using the templates on page 89.

Score the sides of the candle holders and apply slip. Join together the sides and press to make the shape nice and round.

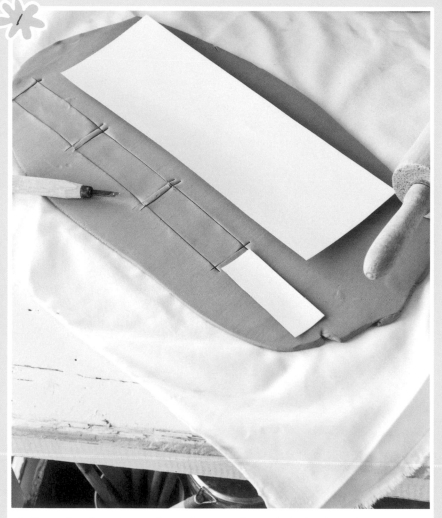

Roll out a slab of clay and cut out stars with a cookie cutter. I used sixteen stars for the candle holder, but the number needed will depend on the size of your cutter.

Roll out the clay, nice and evenly, on a piece of cloth. Place the templates on top and cut out the shapes in the clay. Template number two is for the actual candle holder; make four of these.

Measure where the candle holders should be placed on the bottom slab and score the marked areas. Also score the bottom side of all candle holders and apply slip.

Attach the round candle holders and tidy all joints.

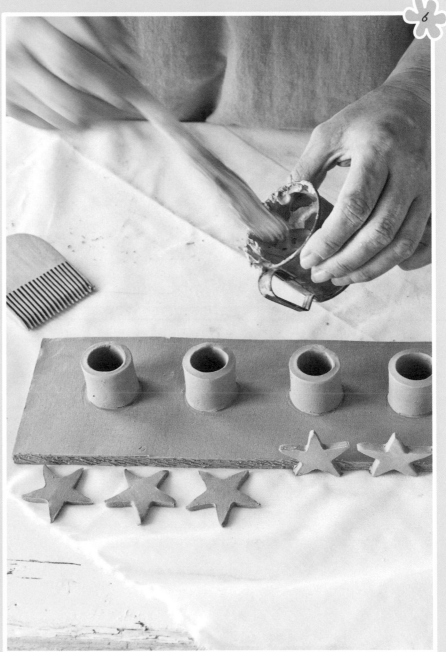

Lay out the stars where they should be attached, score the tips and attach with slip. Cover with plastic wrap and leave to dry slowly.

Advent candle holder template

Here are templates for the star candle holder; you can easily make variations of this by using other cookie cutters. It's also easy to make a round votive for tea lights using the same principle – just leave out the candle holders and instead of the rectangular slab cut out a clay circle.

1 bottom

Make this template x 2

2 candle holder

tip!

Place a few weights inside the candle holder when it is ready so that the bottom does not warp during the drying process.

Bowled over by balloons

Blow up balloons to delight the children,
let kites fly away with the toil of the day.

(from a song by Ramon Anthin)

Eggs galore

One summer our neighbours asked if we would like to have a cockerel. He was a small dwarf bird with no name and lived in their stable following an unfortunate incident in the hen house when he was nearly killed. The hens were nasty and the big cockerel didn't get on with others. The small cockerel couldn't even crow. Our hearts melted when we heard his story. Of course we wanted him!

We converted the old outhouse into a hen house and fenced a large yard with chicken wire. Then the whole family went with great ceremony to pick him up. Carlos. We were given a small dwarf hen as a bonus – Johanna.

The small cockerel got a new lease of life. A yard of his own and a hen. One fine day, we heard a strange noise from the hen yard. Carlos cleared his throat, wheezed a little and then he started. He crowed for an entire day, making up for all the lost cock-a-doodle-doos. We got more hens and chickens who listened to his sweet voice. He lived with us for one year but then he got sick and died. I cried so much that I had to close my little shop that day.

Now we have a new cockerel in the hen house. The hens only lay eggs when they feel like it and sometimes they give up. I wonder if they think about Carlos on those occasions?

Balloons can be used for things other than to delight children. They are perfect for covering with clay to make eggs.

1

Inflate a balloon about half full. Roll out clay and cover the balloon. Carefully press the clay around the balloon.

2

Remove the excess and then tidy the joints with a knife.

3

Tear off tabs around the edge a little unevenly. It should look like a cracked egg. Leave it to dry with the balloon inside. Pierce the balloon when the clay feels sturdy.

Some tips on balloons

Families with young children often have balloons at home. Most of the time we complain about them as they lie dotted around, half punctured. However, balloons are great to use as a mould for pottery.

When you roll out clay and put it around a solid mould, the clay will crack during the drying process unless you remove it from the mould directly. Clay shrinks while it dries whereas your solid mould, such as a bowl, does not. However, if you use a balloon for a mould, the clay will not crack. When the clay shrinks and presses around the balloon, it just changes its shape.

Let's take balloons to a new level. Inflate a balloon about half full or to the size you want. Roll out a thin slab of clay on a piece of cloth. Cover the balloon with the clay. Cut off excess clay and gently cut the edge. I always tear off the edge when I make eggs to get as natural a look as possible. When using a knife, be careful not to puncture the balloon. Leave to dry without plastic. When the clay is so sturdy that it can stand up by itself, you can puncture the balloon.

 White ceramic eggs with daffodils in a birdcage.

 Large egg with crocuses and small bird votives.

 Bowl with eggs. When cutting an even edge with a knife, be careful not to puncture the balloon.

 Small cup, made on a small balloon. Put a clay ring on the bottom and you have a foot. It's easy to roll a handle and attach with some slip.

Make your own »

Make your own

Making votives in different shapes is quick and easy. They also make perfect presents. You can never have too many votives. Templates for the votive and the bird can be found on page 103.

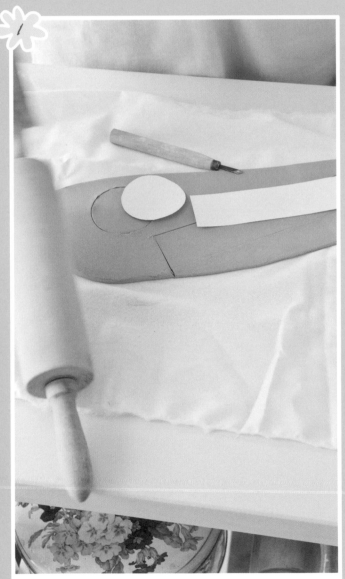

Roll out the clay on a piece of cloth. Place the votive templates on top and cut out the parts in the clay.

Score both the sides and around the bottom part. Apply slip and press together. Tidy the joints.

Roll out another piece of clay. Place the bird template on top, roll it in slightly and lift away.

Score the edges of the votive where the bird should sit and also the bird itself. Apply slip and press together.

4

Cut out the bird in the clay following the shape. Use a sponge to tidy the edges.

Bird votive template

Use the template opposite if you want to make my votive.

A small tea candle is perfect for this size.

The small bird can also be used as an Easter bouquet pendant. Don't forget to make a hole for the string.

side *1*

bottom *2*

bird *3*

tip!
Replace the candle with some candy and use as a bowl!

Glorious gold and silver

Make every day a party, serve morning tea in a gilded cup.

All that glitters is not gold...

I'm like a magpie. Anything that shines and glitters I find irresistible. I like to take it home with me if I can. It doesn't need to be jewellery or anything expensive – gilded frames, old porcelain with gilded edges or glass birds with golden plumes will do just fine.

Unlike magpies, I don't usually fly off with my booty right away – first of all I try to convince the owner that this sparkly stuff would look great at my place. This trick usually works well with mothers-in-law but less so with lords of the manor.

Luckily, my grandparents were missionaries in Ceylon. So I inherited some gilded items, tray tables and trinkets, where no expense was spared in terms of gilding and gold. That suits me just fine!

In this chapter we will travel to the Orient and set the table for a golden party. Welcome!

Bottled gold and silver will complement your pottery, adding an air of luxury and flamboyance.

For circular shapes, use a turntable or banding wheel. Turn whilst holding the brush against the edge.

Paint patterns with a broader brush. Mixing gold and silver produces a striking effect. Small dots run easily. Use only a little gold in your brush and hold the piece horizontally until the dots have dried a little.

Some tips on gold and silver

Gold and silver for pottery, although not the real thing, is still quite costly. Still, a small bottle is enough for a whole bunch of cups and saucers. Paint gold and silver on your finished pottery pieces. They can then be fired in a third firing at up to around 800 degrees. If you want to use decals (see page 24), these can be fired together with the gold.

Do as follows to gild edges. Select a nice piece and put it on a turntable or banding wheel. I always use a brush to gild. Dip the brush carefully in the bottle and put it against the edge of the piece while turning the turntable. If there is too much gold in the brush, the gilded edge will run, which can also look striking.

If you want to make golden dots, hold the piece horizontally and use the tip of a small brush. Remember to use only a little gold in the brush unless you want large dots. Let the gold dry before you put down the piece, to avoid running. I usually use the hairdryer to blow-dry gently from a distance for a little while.

 Set the table with your best pottery for a party.

 Small bowl and cup with decorative golden dots.

 Jug with painted pattern in both gold and silver.

 Small pots with silver edge.

Make your own »

Make your own

A small votive in the shape of a temple is perfect if you want an oriental feel to the table setting. Dip it in your favourite glazing and decorate with gold and silver. Templates can be found on page 117.

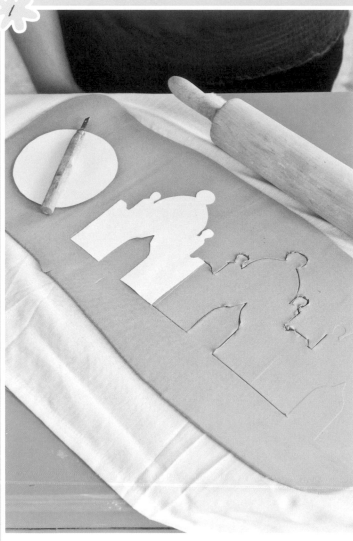

Roll out the clay on a piece of cloth. Turn it several times so the slab is as even as possible. Place template number 1 on the slab and roll it lightly three times in a row. You can now see the design in the clay.

Use a small knife to cut out the contours in the clay. Be careful not to cut off the bud shapes on the temple.

3

Score the bottom and side parts of the temple. Apply slip to the scorings and press together. Tidy the joints with a knife.

4

Finally, wipe a damp sponge over the edges to make sure they are smooth.

115

Follow the step-by-step instructions on the previous page.

temple template

Use the template if you want to make the oriental ceramic votive. Template number 1 should be tripled and cut out in one piece.

1 side

2

bottom

tip!

Make a book end!
Use template 1 and
attach it to a square
bottom slab.

Here are some pieces inspired by a range of flea market bargains. Small plates, soup plates, cake tin, butter dish made of pressed glass, plastic tray, bread basket and glass bowls.

Flea market inspiration

Give in to the temptation of a roadside sign. Perhaps you'll find a bargain, or maybe just travel back in time a little.

Fabulous finds by the roadside

Flea market signs always crop up in the summer. Every mile or so, these lovely handwritten signs will entice you into a garage or a barn. I find it so hard to drive past them, thinking there might be something on a shelf or in a box that I risk missing. So I almost always stop and run in quickly to get a general idea of what's on offer. Usually I'll dig around some boxes and leaf through a few books. Then I run out again, rarely empty-handed. A bowl or perhaps a pair of candlesticks have become mine for a pittance. Flea markets should be cheap; that's the whole point and it's absolutely necessary if, like me, you stop at every single one.

My favourite flea market is located in the neighbouring village. It is absolutely cluttered with stuff. It doesn't matter how many times I've been there, I discover new things and even whole new sections every time. As I stroll around in there, time stands still. I lift up dainty crystal glasses, caress linen tablecloths and try to decipher porcelain stamps and artists' signatures. Chat with the old flea market man about the weather and drink a soft drink through a straw. Obviously I always find something. My home these days is full of great flea market finds. So many of them that soon I might very well put a sign out by the roadside myself.

At the flea market you can find lots of pretty moulds for a pittance. Perfect to use for pottery.

Use an aluminium cake tin. Roll out the clay on a piece of cloth. Cover the outside of the tin with plastic wrap and then with clay, using a sponge to press it into place. Cut the edge.

Let the clay dry before you carefully lift the tin off.

Some tips on flea market finds

There is no limit to how much fun you can have with flea market finds. I usually keep my eyes open for pieces with pretty shapes or patterns. A lot of bowls and plates made of pressed glass have patterns on the outside surface. Put clay over these and press and you have a ceramic bowl with a beautiful pattern on the inside. Trays, pots and ashtrays are perfect to use as moulds.

There are also lots of tools for the pottery workshop that can be bought at flea markets. Have a look among the household goods for rolling pins and knives. There is usually an abundance of chains and keys, which leave nice patterns in clay.

On the next page, there are some more inspirational tips on what to do with flea market finds. Here is what to do. Always cover the mould with plastic before applying the clay. If you want to make a bowl, it is easier to shape the clay inside the mould, leave it to dry and then lift it out. If you apply clay on the outside of a mould, remember that clay shrinks during the drying process but the mould does not. So you must always remove your clay piece after a while once it feels sturdy, otherwise it will crack. Leave it to dry under plastic.

 The bottom of an aspic dish is used to make the shape of the pretty little plates that look like flowers. The other plates are rolled out and shaped using old plates.

 Make a sponge cake using your own ceramic mould. I used an aluminium cake tin found at a flea market as a mould.

 A basket for fermenting bread becomes the mould for a pretty ceramic bowl with an unusual design.

 You can find loads of pressed glass for a pittance; use the pieces as moulds for your pottery. Here is a small square mould which is great for tea balls.

Make your own »

Make your own

Here I show you how to use a tray found at a flea market to make your own ceramic tray. I have used a rectangular plastic tray. Follow my step-by-step instructions. Templates for the handles and edge decoration are on page 131.

Cover the inside of the tray with plastic foil and press the clay down using a sponge.

Roll out the clay on a piece of cloth, nice and evenly. Put the tray on the clay and cut following the edge of the tray.

Roll out some more clay and cut out handles and the edge decoration using the template.

Mark the area where the handles should be and score both the tray and the handles. Apply slip and press together.

Repeat the process for the edge decoration and attach.

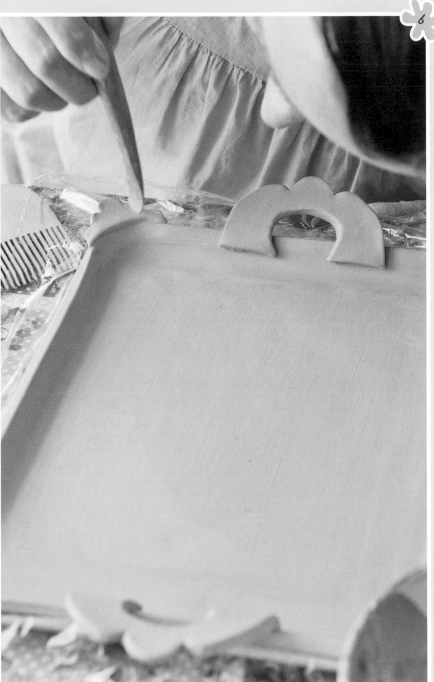

Tidy all joints and the edge with a sponge. Leave to dry under plastic wrap. Put a few flat weights on the tray so that it does not warp during the drying process.

Follow the step-by-step instructions on the previous page.

tray template

Here are templates for a tray with handles and decoration.
A round tray will look just as nice.

tip!

It isn't difficult to draw your own decorations for the tray. Make your own template by sketching a shape on paper and cutting it out. Place it on the rolled-out clay and cut out the template in the clay. Score and attach to the tray with slip.

Handles

Edge decoration

132

Adhesives and cheating

A toad sits in the shade.

Sometimes he jumps up into the bowl to cool down in the water.

But mostly he just sits there.

Waiting to be kissed by a passer-by who doesn't know that only frogs can turn into princes.

Clever cheats

Now we come to the delicate topic of cheating – topic I love. It is my strong conviction that as long as it is done with aesthetic sense and feeling, cheating in all forms is permitted.

Even if I dislike the word cheating when it comes to pottery, it is hard to draw a line between what is really cheating and what is not. Many probably think that pre-mixed glazes, decals and adhesives definitely fall into the category of cheating. I just think they are perfect aids to achieve the result I want.

It is very personal and difficult to decide what constitutes cheating in other modern art forms as well. I don't think an artist is cheating when he or she makes a collage of pictures painted by somebody else. Nor are the photographer's filters, developing or retouching techniques cheating. A composer who uses the computer instead of real instruments is not a cheater either.

I believe that all methods are permitted in the creative process. The results speak for themselves.

This chapter sings the praises of cheating, and I will share my best tips with you. Come along – whether or not you think it's cheating!

psst ...

A strong two-component adhesive is crucial when gluing together ceramic pieces.

Mix the adhesive. Apply the adhesive directly to the pieces you want to attach. Here, a foot will be attached to a plate. Press together and leave to harden. The foot in the foreground is thrown and the one in the background is rolled. A template is available on page 145.

Two-component adhesives, ceramic pieces and metal candle holders.

Glue the decorations using the same method.

Some tips on adhesives and cheating

I use adhesive mainly to attach feet to plates. I find this an easy way to get a good result, since wheel-thrown plates with feet have a tendency to warp during the firing process. Sure, it's a shortcut, but it's actually a durable and good shortcut, provided you use a strong adhesive. My glued plates that I use at home are still in one piece after many years of use.

If you're not afraid of a little cheating, you can also glue decorations to your pottery. The variations are endless because it's possible to mix several types of clay and glazes any way you fancy.

You also won't be limited to ceramic decorations, and will be able to add any material of your choice.

In this chapter I have used candle holders made of metal which I glued to a ceramic bowl. Birds are modelled and attached in the appropriate spot afterwards. Both large and small flowers are rolled out, pressed, built after the glaze firing, and then glued to pots and bowls. On the next page you'll see what it looks like.

Pot with large blue flower as decoration.

Pot with tiny, tiny flowers with blue glazing as edge decor.

A small bird gazes into the water in the bowl.

Candle bowl complete with metal candle holder.

Make your own »

Make your own

Birdbaths look so incredibly lovely in the garden or on the balcony They can even look nice inside, as an adornment along with a winding plant. Follow my step-by-step instructions, throw or roll out a foot and attach it with glue after the firing. The flowers and the bird can be attached afterwards with an adhesive, but here I will attach them directly to show how it is done. You can make each part separately and attach them where you wish. The birdbath will also look good without the foot.

Roll out the clay on a piece of cloth. I used a rusty old lamp shade as a mould. A shallow bowl or a large plate would also work well.

Cover the mould with plastic and press the rolled clay into it using a sponge. Cut off excess clay along the edge.

Roll small balls and shape into a bird. To make the feathers, I flattened a few balls and attached them, overlapping each other.

Score the edge where the bird will sit. Apply slip, attach the bird and press gently.

Roll out some more clay and cut out a couple of flowers using the template.

Score the flowers and middle of the plate where they will be attached, apply slip and press together.

Birdbath template

If you do not have the option of throwing a foot for the birdbath,
there is a template for a rolled foot: see the pictures on page 138.
Score the sides and join together using slip. The small round part
should sit like a lid on top of the foot.

1

small flower

2

large flower

4

lid for foot

3 *side of foot*

tip!

Glue mirror mosaics on the bottom of the plate to make the water reflect.

Moulded magic

There are a lot of stairs in the castle.

If the king gets tired, he can sit down on the landing, break a piece of bread and look out over the water.

It's good to be a king!

Castles in the air

Every time I open the doors of a castle, I feel like I'm travelling back in time. When the doors slam shut behind me, I am back in the castle's heyday when none of the modern conveniences we have these days had found their way into these historical buildings. No lifts. I run up and down the stairs, my heels slam the marble staircase. Sometimes I stop on a landing to catch my breath, look out over the moat and see the ducks floating around like small dots. I run through wings, archways and halls.

I wonder how it was back then. Probably rather cold and grey. Maybe the people who lived in the castle sometimes got lost and met each other on the stairs with flickering candles. Lovebirds probably agreed to meet in a tower to enjoy the view. Not to mention the dinners, with the entire court seated at a long table cluttered with candlelight, treats and roast birds. Beautiful dresses and powdered wigs.

I change directions and continue to run. Can't find my way back, am lost. But it doesn't matter, I don't mind being royal for just a little bit longer.

psst ...

Serving plates are fantastic to use as moulds in pottery and great to store in an old wooden box.

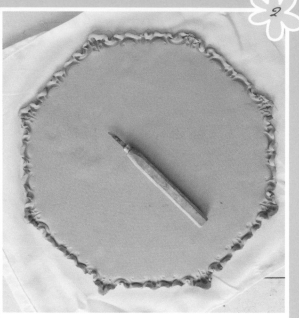

1 Roll out the clay on a piece of cloth. Use a serving plate with a pretty edge decoration and press it upside down on the clay.

2 Lift away the serving plate and cut out the pattern in the clay.

3 Cover the serving plate with a piece of plastic wrap and put the clay inside it. Use a sponge to press against the mould.

Some tips on using plates as moulds

Serving plates make excellent moulds when you want to make beautiful ceramic dishes. All sorts of serving plates can be used. Over time, I have collected beautiful pewter and silver plates. When they are not covered in clay, they are kept in a beautiful wooden box in my workshop and look pretty just where they are.

Here's what to do. Roll out the clay evenly on a piece of cloth. If your plate is very large, it's important to turn the clay several times during the rolling. This makes the clay slab more even. Put your serving plate on the clay and cut out the shape in the clay. If the serving plate has a complex edge decoration, press the serving plate down first, lift away and then cut. This makes it easier to achieve a tidy edge.

Cover the upper side of the serving plate with a piece of plastic wrap. Place the cut-out clay inside the plate and press down with a sponge. You can also roll out the decoration separately and attach it to the plate afterwards, and there are endless variations.

Cover with plastic and leave the plate with the clay until it has dried completely. Unless you place a few weights to hold the clay in place during the drying process, there is a big danger that your piece will warp.

In the chapter Adhesives and Cheating, you will find information on how to make feet for your plates.

 Inside a burnt-down orangery, an olive tree and a small candle plate provide decoration.

 A small, footed plate with a pretty glass dome.

 Red onions on a plate with a pattern from a crocheted tablecloth.

 Oblong serving plates were used as moulds for these sconces.

Make your own »

Make your own

The sconces look nice and even quite complicated, but they are not difficult to make at all. Follow my step-by-step instructions. Templates are on page 159.

Press the clay into the mould using a sponge.

Roll out some clay on a piece of cloth, nice and evenly. I used a rather large oblong serving plate as a mould. Put the plate on the clay and cut out the shape in the clay.

Roll out a long slab of clay and cut out the edge decoration using the template. Cut out the pieces for the candle holder.

Score the area on the plate where the decor will be attached and the reverse of the decoration. Apply slip and press together. Tidy the edge with a sponge.

You can use the same decoration for the candle holder as for the edge of the plate. Score and apply slip on all parts to be attached. Lastly, put the decoration around the candle holder. Put a small strip of clay below the bottom of the candle holder as support.

Measure and mark where the holder should be attached on the plate to make sure it will sit straight. Attach by scoring and applying slip. Use a bit of folded paper as support under the candle holder while it dries. Cover with plastic wrap and place a few weights on top to prevent the plate from warping.

Follow the step-by-step instructions
on the previous page.

Sconce template

Use a plate that you think will look good as a sconce. I chose an oblong one, but a round one would also look nice.

Do not forget to score all parts that will be attached.

Always use slip, otherwise there is a big danger that the pieces will come apart during the drying process.

1 edge decoration

3 bottom

4 candle holder

2 support

tip!

Measure with a candle to see at what height the candle holder should be attached.

Ugly becomes beautiful

As we all know, beauty is in the eye of the beholder.

Cabinet of shame

Sometimes I make pieces of pottery that I hide once I have removed them from the kiln, pieces which did not turn out at all the way I wanted them. Ugly pieces.

In my workshop I have a large cupboard filled with such pieces, the cabinet of shame. There are lots of shelves next to the cupboard with the finest ceramics, but oddly enough my clients are always attracted to that cupboard. They insist on opening the doors, they root around in the cups and bowls and pull out some sad and ugly piece at the very back which they absolutely must buy.

At this point I usually feel a little ashamed and try to persuade them to select another piece. But they always end up taking home that warped bowl anyway, and perhaps a cup with ugly glazing as well.

I am beginning to understand that what is ugly to me can be pretty to others, and vice versa. That's why I almost never throw away any pieces of pottery.

If the defects are purely aesthetic, I will put the piece in the cupboard, but if a piece has cracked, I usually smash it and save the pieces for future projects.

In this chapter I will show you how ugly can become pretty.

Sometimes things do not turn out the way you wanted.
Sometimes things turn out better than expected.

Save all pieces of pottery that you break or which you think are failures. Smash them into small pieces with a hammer and use for mosaics.

A wooden tray gets new clothes in the form of ceramic mosaics. I mixed both irregular and square pieces of ceramic.

Put small pieces around a candle or inside a pot as decoration.

Some tips on how ugly can become beautiful

Sure, it's disappointing when you realize a piece of pottery did not turn out the way you wanted it as you remove it from the kiln. Not to mention when you drop a favourite cup on the floor. Try to think of new possibilities for the faulty piece to avoid throwing it away. With a little imagination, you may even improve the piece!

Sometimes when I open the kiln too quickly, the glazing cracks. I find it very pretty. Even if I can't sell the pieces in a shop, I still find the mesh pattern of the cracked surface so beautiful. Once I put blueberries in a bowl with cracked glazing, and the blueberry juices settled in the cracks and left a fabulous purple pattern.

You can go a long way with a hammer, nippers and a drill. Adhesive, tile adhesive, silver chains and candle grease will take you even further.

Collect pieces of pottery that you are not happy with in a basket until you have figured out what you want to do with them.

 You can make jewellery with pottery shards. The picture shows earrings, rings, bracelets and pendants for necklaces made of pottery shards. You will find plenty of materials for making jewellery in hobby shops. Cut out a shape with nippers and rub the sharp edges with sandpaper. Drill a small hole in the shard or glue a mount to it with superglue.

 A teacup with decals fell to the floor and broke into pieces.

 One of the shards lives on in the form of a nice ring. Other shards became a pair of unique earrings with roses.

 Mixing jewellery made of pottery shards with other silver jewellery can look stylish.

Make your own »

Votives

A bunch of faulty cups. Handles that break, a crack in the glazing, chipped or warped. Instead of throwing them in the bin, I fill them with candle wax. Buy a box of candle wax and melt in a water bath. Put a candlewick in each cup, pour in the candle wax and let it solidify. On a tray, the cups look like a pretty still life picture and spread a warm glow.

Flower pot

The bottom of the bowl was severely cracked in the kiln. Using it for food is out of the question unless you want a stained tablecloth. Instead, plant a flower in the bowl and put it on a plate. Cracks in the bottom of pieces of pottery are not unusual. Sometimes you will also make the bottom of a cup or bowl too thin and then unintentionally cut off a part of it with the cutting wire. All these pieces are perfect for growing plants in, since they have natural draining holes.

Plate for vegetables

A luxurious plate for vegetables with gilded details is the result of the piece drying too fast, which left a couple of cracks on the edge. What a stroke of luck! Brush on some gold to instantly make the cracks decorative. Most defects on pieces of pottery can be camouflaged with gold or silver – a quick and easy way to turn something ugly into something beautiful and lavish. Read more about gold in the Chapter Glorious Gold and Silver, page 107.

Plate with decoration

Sometimes I open the kiln only to discover that the glazing does not look anything like what I had intended. The glazing might be scratched or matt here and there. It might be runny, or a particle or chip from the kiln might have got stuck in the glaze during firing. In cases like these it's time to get your decals out. Soak them in water and apply them over the areas you dislike. Fire once more. Now you can put that bowl on your display shelf. Read more about decals in the chapter Discovering Decals, page 23.

Fabulous Pottery

Frida Anthin Broberg

I incorporated my initials when I created my company name. It reflects my view on pottery so well. I want the pieces I create to be fabulous, light-hearted, playful and beautiful.

After five years of studying at four art schools, I am a trained crafts teacher but I work full-time as a potter. Of all the art forms I have tried, none competes with pottery, and the pleasure and joy I experience when I create clay pottery is never-ending.

I often put aesthetics before technique when I work with pottery, and perhaps my methods might be seen as a little newfangled since I am not scared of shortcuts or cheating.

Frida Anthin Broberg
www.fabkeramik.se

Some facts

All material used in this book can be purchased from your nearest clay wholesale supplier.

The clay used in all the step-by-step pictures is white burning stoneware clay with 25% chamotte.

White, black and red burning pottery and stoneware clay were used in the other photographs.

I bisque-fire my pieces of pottery at a little over 900 degrees and then glaze-fire them at up to 1200 degrees, depending on the type of clay I use.

All the pieces of pottery in this book have been dipped in the same white glaze; in some chapters the white glaze has been stained with a colour.

In the chapter on engobe, I used engobe powder in different colours mixed with water.

In order to follow the step-by-step instructions in this book, you will need a rolling pin and cotton cloth to roll the clay on, a knife to cut shapes using templates, a fork to score pieces to be joined together, a sponge to tidy up with and some plastic wrap. You won't need much more than that in terms of tools.

Slip is a word frequently used in this book. In fact, slip is quite simply watered-down clay, which is used as a glue to hold clay pieces together.

Read the glossary on the next page if there are any words you are not familiar with.

Glossary

Chamotte
Particles of fired clay. Mixed with clay to improve structural strength.

Decals
Ready-made designs to put on the fired piece of pottery which are then burnt in a kiln and become permanent.

To throw on a wheel
A technique used to create round pieces, such as bowls. The potter places the clay on a rotating table (a turntable) and shapes the clay with their hands.

Engobe
Clay slurry with or without staining. Used to decorate pieces of pottery. Engobe is applied on leather-hard clay before bisque firing.

Glaze
Coating on ceramics making the items waterproof. Glaze is available in all colours and with different effects. When the ceramic object is bisque-fired, it is dipped in a glaze and fired again at a higher temperature, adapted to the glaze.

Turntable
Manual rotating worktop.

Earthenware clay
Earthenware clay is fired at a low temperature and is the oldest material used in pottery.

Leather-hard clay
Clay when it has been partially dried, enough to be able to be handled without being deformed.

Handle
A handle on a cup, for example.

Scoring
Creating a rough structure on a surface.

Bisque firing
The first firing of a ceramic object. Generally ceramic objects are fired twice.

Slip
Clay glue. Water-soaked clay with a thick consistency, used to join parts.

Stoneware clay
Tolerates a higher temperature than earthenware and can be fired until it sinters, in other words until it becomes waterproof.

Sponge-stick
A small sponge attached to a stick.

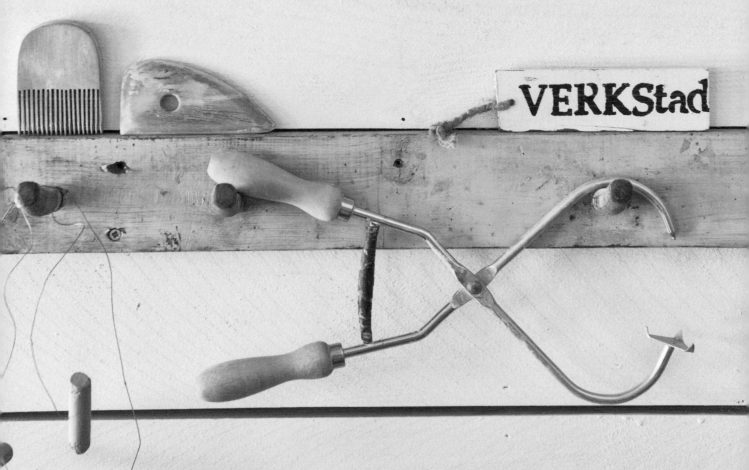

tools

There are lots of different tools for clay and pottery. Often you can just as easily use what you can find in your kitchen drawers, but I use the following tools almost daily in my workshop.

 Sponge-stick

 Throwing ribs

 Brushes

 Sponge

 Rolling pin

 Modelling sticks

 Knife

 Mirettes

 Scriber

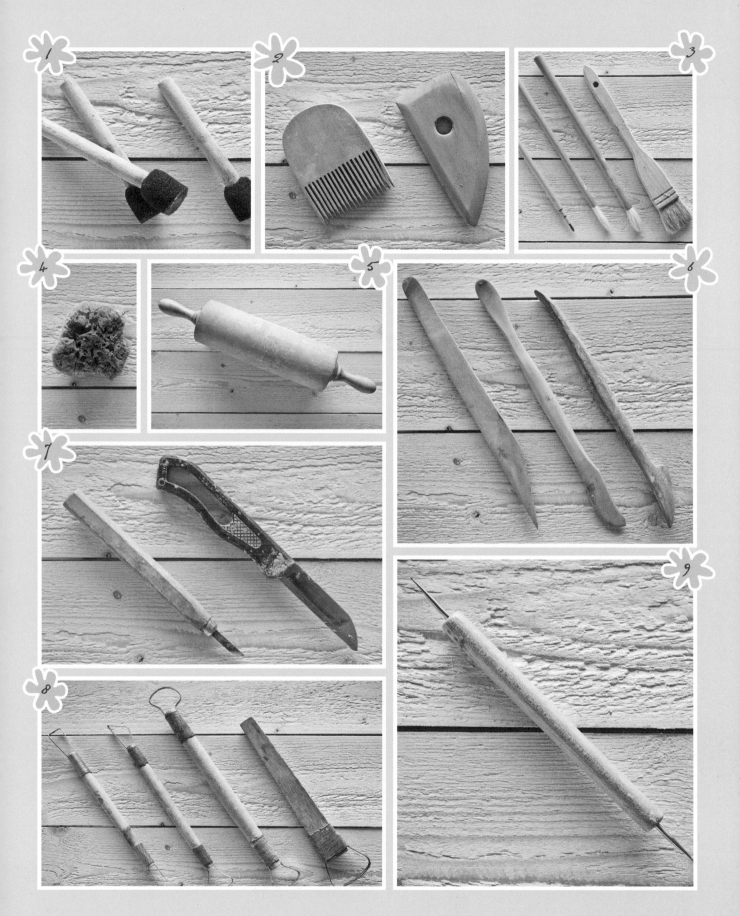

thank you!

Tukan förlag

Andreas Hylthén, for all the long days spent in the field and all the fantastic photos

Sofia Brolin, for designing with a steady hand

Johanna Mattsson, for the idea

Elisabeth Kreivi, my sounding board and mentor

Maria Kron, for all the props and feedback

Family and friends

Jack and Bill

Sebastian, there would be no book without you

We photographed at the following locations
My workshop and my house
Örebro castle
Karlslund
Rönne trädgård
Elisabeth Kreivi's home
Krons house at Gålsjö

Props from
Rönne trädgård
Zaga design
Maria Kron
Johanna Mattsson
Maria Klasson

Models
Johanna Mattsson
Britta the bulldog

Index

Notes

A DAVID & CHARLES BOOK
© Tukan förlag 2011
www.tukanforlag.se

David & Charles is an imprint of F&W Media International, Ltd
Brunel House, Forde Close, Newton Abbot, TQ12 4PU, UK

F&W Media International, Ltd is a subsidiary of F+W Media, Inc
10151 Carver Road, Suite #200, Blue Ash, OH 45242, USA

First published in the UK and USA in 2013
Originally published in Sweden as *Fabulös Keramik*

Frida Anthin Broberg has asserted her right to be identified as author of this work in accordance with the Copyright, Designs and Patents Act, 1988.

A catalogue record for this book is available from the British Library.

ISBN-13: 978-1-4463-0346-7 paperback
ISBN-10: 1-4463-0346-2 paperback

Printed in China by RR Donnelley for:
F&W Media International, Ltd
Brunel House, Forde Close, Newton Abbot, TQ12 4PU, UK

10 9 8 7 6 5 4 3 2 1

Text, pottery and styling: Frida Anthin Broberg
Photos: Andreas Hylthén
Graphic design: Sofia Brolin
Artwork: Vitpunkt

F+W Media publishes high quality books on a wide range of subjects.
For more great book ideas visit: **www.stitchcraftcreate.co.uk**